Raising Resilient ADHD Teen Boys:

9 Solutions for Parenting Teen Boys with Strength and Compassion

I Booky

ABOUT THE AUTHOR

Does parenting have to involve headaches, shouting, anger, or sadness, even over minor hiccups? Absolutely not!

With I Booky's guidance, parenting becomes a journey of discovery and joy. I Booky's books serve as a beacon of support, offering practical advice and heartfelt insights into the art of raising your children. Emphasizing discipline, empathy, and humor, and addressing the needs of special children and teenagers, I Booky empowers you to navigate the parenting journey with confidence.

Join I Booky in transforming the parenting experience—one page, one moment, one child at a time.

Table of contents

Introduction

- **Understanding ADHD in Teen Boys**
- **The Importance of Resilience in Parenting**

Introduction

In the unpredictable voyage of parenthood, each family charts a unique course through the challenges and triumphs that accompany raising teenage boys. The canvas of adolescence is vast, painted with moments of joy, confusion, and growth. When Attention Deficit Hyperactivity Disorder (ADHD) becomes a part of this narrative, the journey takes on an additional layer of complexity, demanding resilience, understanding, and unwavering compassion.

The teenage years are a pivotal chapter, marked by rapid changes in physical, emotional, and social spheres. ADHD introduces its unique set of challenges, influencing academic pursuits, social dynamics, and self-perception. This introduction serves as our launchpad into the heart of these complexities, acknowledging the diversity of experiences while recognizing the common thread that ties all parents of ADHD teens together.

Parenting, even without the nuances of ADHD, is an ever-evolving dance. With ADHD in the mix, it becomes a dance of resilience, where every misstep is an opportunity to learn, adapt, and grow. Resilience is not just a quality; it's a skill that transforms challenges into stepping stones, allowing families to navigate the peaks and valleys of adolescence with grace and understanding.

Understanding ADHD in teen boys

Understanding ADHD in teen boys is a crucial aspect of navigating the challenges and complexities that arise during adolescence. ADHD, or Attention Deficit Hyperactivity Disorder, is a neurodevelopmental condition that affects a person's ability to focus, control impulses, and regulate energy levels. In the teenage years, these challenges can manifest in various aspects of their lives, influencing academic performance, social interactions, and emotional well-being.

Teenagers with ADHD often find themselves grappling with the demands of the academic environment. The traditional structure of classrooms and the need for sustained attention can pose significant hurdles. It's essential to recognize that the academic struggles faced by teens with ADHD are not indicative of a lack of intelligence or effort. Rather, ADHD shapes how they process information and engage with academic tasks, necessitating tailored support and understanding from parents and educators.

Social dynamics become intricate during adolescence, and for teens with ADHD, navigating friendships and relationships can be particularly challenging. Impulsivity and difficulties with social cues may contribute to social difficulties. Recognizing the impact of ADHD on social interactions allows parents to provide guidance and support, fostering the development of essential social skills.

The emotional rollercoaster of adolescence is intensified for teens with ADHD. Emotional regulation, a skill that develops gradually, can be especially challenging for these individuals. Understanding that mood swings, frustration, and impulsive reactions are often linked to ADHD allows parents to approach emotional challenges with empathy and patience.

Building emotional resilience involves equipping teens with coping mechanisms, teaching stress management techniques, and providing a supportive environment where mistakes are viewed as opportunities for growth.

Crucially, it's important to acknowledge that ADHD is not a one-size-fits-all condition. Each teen with ADHD is unique, with their strengths and challenges. Understanding these individual differences allows parents to celebrate the strengths of their teen boys, fostering a positive self-image and creating an environment where they can thrive.

In essence, understanding ADHD in teen boys goes beyond recognizing it as a neurodevelopmental condition. It involves acknowledging the specific ways in which ADHD influences their daily lives, from academics to social interactions and emotional well-being. By understanding the intricacies of ADHD in the context of adolescence, parents can provide the necessary support and guidance, creating an environment where their teen boys can navigate the challenges of this transformative period with resilience and confidence.

The Importance of Resilience in Parenting

Parenting is a journey filled with joy, wonder, and the unexpected. It's a complex dance where each step requires adaptability, patience, and unwavering love. However, when parenting involves children with special needs, such as Attention Deficit Hyperactivity Disorder (ADHD), the dance takes on a unique rhythm. In this context, the importance of resilience in parenting becomes not just a desirable trait but an essential tool for guiding families through the complexities of raising children with compassion and fortitude.

Resilience in parenting is the ability to bounce back from difficulties, adapt to changes, and face challenges with courage and strength. It provides a crucial foundation for navigating the unpredictable nature of parenting, particularly when raising children with ADHD. This essay explores the multifaceted significance of resilience, examining how it helps parents adapt to the unpredictable, cultivate patience and empathy, turn challenges into opportunities, and serves as a powerful model for children.

Adapting to the Unpredictable:

Parenting, by its nature, is inherently unpredictable. Each child is a unique individual, and when ADHD is part of the equation, the challenges become even more varied. Resilience allows parents to adapt to ever-changing circumstances, recognizing that flexibility is a key component of effective parenting. Children with ADHD may present challenges in areas such as organization, time management, and emotional regulation. Resilient parents view these challenges as opportunities for growth and learning, understanding that setbacks are a natural part of the parenting journey.

Cultivating Patience and Empathy:

Patience and empathy are integral components of resilience in parenting. Children with ADHD may require additional time, understanding, and support. Resilient parents approach moments of frustration with patience, recognizing that their child's struggles are not intentional but are part of the neurodevelopmental aspects of ADHD. Empathy plays a crucial role in resilience, allowing parents to see the world through their child's eyes and fostering a deeper connection that enables effective support.

Turning Challenges into Opportunities:

Resilient parenting involves reframing challenges as opportunities for growth. Instead of viewing obstacles as insurmountable, resilient parents see them as chances to build coping skills, problem-solving abilities, and emotional resilience in their children. This perspective shift is transformative, instilling a sense of optimism and adaptability in both parent and child. Children with ADHD often face societal misconceptions and stigmas. Resilient parents become advocates for their children, working to dispel misunderstandings and promote a more inclusive and understanding community.

Modeling Resilience for Children:

Perhaps one of the most powerful aspects of resilient parenting is its impact on children. Children learn by example, and parents who exhibit resilience in the face of challenges provide a valuable lesson for their children. By demonstrating how to navigate difficulties with courage and grace, resilient parents equip their children with the tools necessary to face life's challenges independently. This modeling of resilience becomes a powerful form of guidance, shaping the child's worldview and instilling a sense of inner strength.

In conclusion, the importance of resilience in parenting, particularly when raising children with ADHD, is evident in its multifaceted role. Resilience allows parents to adapt to the unpredictable, cultivate patience and empathy, turn challenges into opportunities, and serve as a powerful model for children. It transforms the parenting journey from a series of obstacles into a path of growth, connection, and shared resilience. In navigating the dance of parenting, resilience emerges as the steadfast partner, guiding families through the complexities with grace and strength.

Part One: Navigating ADHD in the Teen Years

- Recognizing ADHD Challenges in Adolescence

-Impact on Academic Performance and Social Relationships

Part One: Navigating ADHD in the Teen Years

Navigating Attention Deficit Hyperactivity Disorder (ADHD) during adolescence is a unique journey for parents and teens. This transformative period, marked by physical, emotional, and social changes, demands a nuanced approach. Understanding the impact of ADHD during these years is crucial.

In academics, teens with ADHD face heightened pressures. Collaboration between parents and educators is key, involving personalized plans and a supportive environment. Socially, intricate dynamics challenge friendships, requiring social skills training and fostering inclusivity. Emotionally, the amplified rollercoaster necessitates coping mechanisms and open communication.

Encouraging independence involves empowering teens to manage strengths and challenges. Fostering a positive self-image is crucial, addressing potential self-esteem issues. In conclusion, navigating ADHD in the teen years requires understanding, collaboration, and tailored strategies for academic, social, and emotional well-being.

Recognizing ADHD Challenges in Adolescence

Adolescence, a period of tumultuous growth and self-discovery, poses distinctive challenges for individuals grappling with Attention Deficit Hyperactivity Disorder (ADHD). Understanding and recognizing these challenges are paramount for fostering an environment that supports the unique needs of adolescents with ADHD. The multifaceted nature of these challenges encompasses academic, social, emotional, and behavioral dimensions.

Academic Challenges:

1. Sustained Attention Demands: Adolescents with ADHD often grapple with sustaining attention during extended periods, impacting their engagement in class discussions, the completion of assignments, and overall academic performance.

2. Organizational Struggles: Challenges in organizational skills and time management may lead to missed deadlines and difficulties in maintaining an orderly approach to academic responsibilities, exacerbating stress levels.

3. Impulsivity in Learning: Impulsivity can disrupt the learning process, causing hasty decision-making and hindering the absorption of complex concepts, potentially affecting comprehension and retention.

Social Challenges:

1. Navigating Peer Relationships: The intricacies of forming and sustaining friendships can be complicated by impulsivity and social cue misinterpretation, potentially leading to isolation or strained relationships.

2. Communication Hurdles: Expressing thoughts and emotions coherently may present challenges, impacting effective communication with peers and adults and potentially contributing to misunderstandings.

3. Self-Esteem Erosion: Academic and social difficulties can take a toll on self-esteem, fostering negative self-perception and potentially leading to feelings of inadequacy or isolation.

Emotional Regulation:

1. Intense Emotional Responses: Adolescents with ADHD may experience heightened emotional responses, struggling to regulate emotions appropriately, leading to intense reactions to everyday stressors.

2. Frustration and Impatience: The difficulty in managing frustration and impatience can manifest in emotional outbursts, disrupting interpersonal relationships and adding to the emotional complexity of adolescence.

3. Stress Management Struggles: Coping with stress may prove challenging, requiring tailored strategies to manage anxiety and avoid becoming overwhelmed by the increasing demands of adolescence.

Behavioral Challenges:

1. Impulsivity's Impact: Impulsive actions may manifest in risky behaviors, affecting decision-making and potentially exposing adolescents to avoidable dangers or conflicts.

2. Hyperactivity's Influence: Restlessness and hyperactivity can interfere with tasks requiring sustained attention, potentially hindering academic progress and contributing to feelings of frustration.

3. Initiation Hurdles: Starting tasks independently may be an ongoing challenge, affecting the initiation and completion of assignments, chores, or projects.

Identification and Intervention:

1. Observational Awareness: Caregivers and educators should maintain a heightened awareness, observing academic performance, social interactions, and behavioral patterns indicative of ADHD challenges.

2. Communication Bridge: Establishing open lines of communication with the adolescent is fundamental, fostering an environment where they feel comfortable expressing their experiences, challenges, and emotional states.

3. Professional Assessment: Seeking a professional assessment from healthcare providers or educational psychologists facilitates an accurate diagnosis, paving the way for tailored intervention strategies.

The impact of Attention Deficit Hyperactivity Disorder (ADHD) on academic performance and social relationships is profound, shaping the experiences of individuals in both educational and interpersonal settings. Understanding these effects is essential for devising strategies to support those with ADHD effectively.

Impact on Academic Performance and Social Relationships

Impact on Academic Performance

1. Difficulty Sustaining Attention: One of the core challenges of ADHD is sustaining attention over extended periods. This difficulty can lead to distractibility, frequent task-switching, and challenges in focusing on academic assignments, resulting in decreased overall academic performance.

2. Organizational Struggles: Individuals with ADHD often face challenges in organizational skills and time management. This can manifest as difficulties in planning, completing assignments, and keeping track of deadlines, affecting the quality and timely submission of academic work.

3. Impulsivity in Learning: Impulsive behaviors may interfere with the learning process. Students with ADHD may struggle with impulse control, answering questions hastily, or making quick decisions without fully considering the consequences, impacting their understanding and retention of information.

4. **Inconsistent Performance:** The variability in attention and focus levels can lead to inconsistent academic performance. On days when symptoms are more pronounced, individuals with ADHD may struggle to perform at their full potential, creating a pattern of unpredictability.

Impact on Social Relationships:

1. **Navigating Friendships:** Forming and maintaining friendships can be challenging for individuals with ADHD due to impulsivity, difficulties in reading social cues, and managing interpersonal interactions. This can result in social isolation or strained relationships.

2. **Communication Difficulties:** Expressing thoughts coherently and listening actively can be hindered by impulsivity and distractibility. This may lead to misunderstandings in conversations, impacting the quality of social interactions.

3. Emotional Sensitivity: ADHD can contribute to heightened emotional responses, making individuals more sensitive to social cues and interactions. This emotional intensity may impact how they perceive and react to social situations, influencing relationship dynamics.

4. Peer Acceptance: The challenges associated with ADHD may lead to difficulties in gaining peer acceptance. Misunderstandings about impulsive behavior or academic struggles can contribute to a sense of exclusion or stigma.

5. Self-Esteem Impact: Academic challenges and social difficulties can have a direct impact on self-esteem. Individuals with ADHD may develop negative self-perceptions, feeling inadequate or different from their peers.

Intervention Strategies:

1. Individualized Academic Support: Tailored academic support, such as personalized learning plans, additional time for assignments, or specialized teaching methods, can mitigate the impact of ADHD on academic performance.

2. Executive Functioning Training: Interventions focusing on developing organizational and time-management skills can enhance an individual's ability to navigate academic responsibilities more effectively.

3. Social Skills Training: Programs designed to improve social skills, communication, and impulse control can aid individuals with ADHD in navigating social relationships more successfully.

4. Counseling and Support Groups: Emotional support through counseling or participation in support groups can provide individuals with ADHD a space to address the emotional impact of academic and social challenges.

Understanding the impact of ADHD on academic performance and social relationships allows for targeted interventions. By combining academic support, executive functioning training, and social skills development, individuals with ADHD can overcome challenges, build resilience, and thrive in both academic and interpersonal spheres.

Part Two: Building a Foundation of Understanding

- Educating Yourself and Others about ADHD

- Fostering Open Communication with Your Teen

Part Two: Building a Foundation of Understanding

Building a foundation of understanding about Attention Deficit Hyperactivity Disorder (ADHD) is crucial for individuals, families, educators, and communities. By fostering awareness and knowledge about ADHD, we can create a supportive environment that recognizes the unique needs of those with ADHD. This foundation serves as a starting point for informed decision-making, effective interventions, and the promotion of inclusivity.

Understanding ADHD:

1. Neurobiological Basis: ADHD is rooted in neurobiological factors, affecting the brain's executive functions responsible for attention, impulse control, and self-regulation. Recognizing ADHD as a neurodevelopmental disorder is essential for dispelling misconceptions about laziness or lack of willpower.

2. Heterogeneity of Presentation: ADHD manifests in diverse ways. While commonly associated with hyperactivity, it also presents as inattention or impulsivity. Understanding this heterogeneity is crucial for recognizing the varying challenges individuals may face.

3. Developmental Continuum: ADHD is not solely a childhood disorder; it often persists into adolescence and adulthood. Acknowledging ADHD as a lifelong condition facilitates early intervention, ongoing support, and a more nuanced understanding of its impact across the lifespan.

Impact on Daily Life:

1. Academic Challenges: ADHD can affect academic performance due to difficulties in sustained attention, organization, and time management. Recognizing these challenges enables the implementation of tailored strategies, such as individualized learning plans and accommodations.

2. Social Dynamics: Impulsivity and difficulties in social cues may impact peer relationships. Acknowledging these challenges fosters a supportive environment that encourages social skills training, peer understanding, and inclusivity.

3. Emotional Regulation: Individuals with ADHD may experience heightened emotional responses. Understanding the impact on emotional regulation promotes the development of coping mechanisms and empathy within relationships.

Building Empathy:

1. Dispelling Myths and Stigma: Education about ADHD helps dispel myths and reduce stigma. Recognizing ADHD as a neurobiological condition emphasizes the need for empathy and understanding rather than judgment.

2. Appreciating Strengths: Individuals with ADHD often possess unique strengths, such as creativity, resilience, and hyperfocus. Building an understanding that ADHD is not solely a deficit but a different cognitive style encourages appreciation for these strengths.

Effective Interventions:

1. Early Identification: Recognizing ADHD early allows for timely intervention and support. This may involve professional assessments, collaboration between educators and parents, and individualized strategies to address academic and behavioral challenges.

2. Tailored Educational Approaches: Understanding diverse learning styles and needs enables educators to implement tailored approaches, creating an inclusive learning environment that supports individuals with ADHD.

3. Family and Community Support: Building a foundation of understanding extends to families and communities.

Support groups, workshops, and open communication channels foster a collective commitment to embracing and supporting individuals with ADHD.

Educating Yourself and Others about ADHD

Educating yourself and others about Attention Deficit Hyperactivity Disorder (ADHD) is a powerful step toward fostering awareness and building a supportive environment. Recognizing the nuances of ADHD and its impact on individuals' lives enables empathy and informed decision-making.

Self-Education:

1. Understand the Basics: Learn about the neurobiological basis of ADHD, including its diverse presentations such as inattention, hyperactivity, and impulsivity.

2. Explore Academic Impacts: Gain insights into how ADHD affects academic performance, including challenges in sustained attention, organization, and time management.

3. Appreciate Emotional Dynamics: Explore the emotional aspects of ADHD, including heightened emotional responses and difficulties in emotional regulation.

Educating Others:

1. Dispel Myths: Share accurate information to dispel common myths and misconceptions about ADHD, emphasizing its neurodevelopmental nature.

2. Highlight Strengths: Emphasize the unique strengths associated with ADHD, such as creativity, resilience, and hyperfocus.

3. Promote Empathy: Encourage empathy by fostering an understanding of the challenges individuals with ADHD face in daily life, both academically and socially.

Practical Steps:

1. Attend Workshops and Webinars: Participate in workshops or webinars to deepen your understanding of ADHD and learn about effective strategies for support.

2. Access Reliable Resources: Utilize reputable resources such as books, articles, and websites dedicated to ADHD education and advocacy.

3. Seek Professional Guidance: Consult healthcare professionals or specialists for personalized information and guidance on managing ADHD.

Advocacy and Support:

1. Open Communication: Foster open communication within families, schools, and communities to create a supportive network for individuals with ADHD.

2. Advocate for Inclusive Practices: Encourage inclusive practices in educational settings, workplaces, and community spaces to accommodate the needs of individuals with ADHD.

3. Participate in Support Groups: Join or facilitate support groups for individuals with ADHD and their families, providing a platform for shared experiences and mutual support.

By educating yourself and others about ADHD, you contribute to a more understanding and inclusive society. This knowledge empowers individuals with ADHD to navigate challenges with resilience while promoting a culture of empathy and support.

Fostering Open Communication with Your Teen

Building and maintaining open communication with your teenager is essential for fostering a healthy parent-teen relationship. Adolescence is a time of significant change, and open communication provides a foundation for understanding, trust, and mutual support. Here are key strategies to promote open communication with your teen:

1. Create a Judgment-Free Zone: Ensure your teen feels safe expressing themselves without fear of judgment. Avoid criticism and instead, offer constructive feedback when necessary.

2. Listen Actively: Practice active listening by giving your full attention when your teen speaks. This includes making eye contact, nodding, and providing verbal cues to show you are engaged.

3. Express Empathy: Demonstrate empathy by acknowledging your teen's feelings and perspectives. Validate their emotions even if you may not fully agree with their viewpoint.

4. Be Approachable: Maintain an approachable demeanor. Let your teen know that they can come to you with any concerns or questions without fear of reprisal.

5. Set Aside Quality Time: Schedule regular one-on-one time with your teen. Whether it's a designated dinner, a walk, or a shared activity, this time provides a relaxed setting for conversations to unfold.

6. Encourage Open-Ended Questions: Instead of asking yes/no questions, pose open-ended questions that invite your teen to share more about their thoughts and experiences. This fosters deeper conversations.

7. Share Your Experiences: Share relevant aspects of your own life, experiences, and challenges. This can create a sense of mutual sharing and make your teen more comfortable opening up.

8. Respect Their Privacy: Respect your teen's need for privacy. While open communication is crucial, it's equally important to recognize and honor their personal space.

9. Discuss Difficult Topics with Sensitivity: Approach sensitive or challenging topics with care. Choose appropriate times for discussions and ensure a non-confrontational environment.

10. Model Healthy Communication: Demonstrate healthy communication within your own relationships. Your teen learns valuable communication skills by observing how you navigate conversations.

Fostering open communication with your teen is an ongoing process that requires patience, empathy, and a commitment to building a trusting relationship. By creating an environment where your teen feels heard and valued, you contribute to their emotional well-being and the overall strength of your parent-teen bond.

Part Three: Strength-Based Parenting
  - Identifying and Cultivating Your Teen's Strengths
  - Encouraging a Positive Self-Image

Part Three: Strength-Based Parenting

Parenting is a dynamic journey marked by diverse philosophies, each influencing the development of a child in unique ways. Among these approaches, strength-based parenting stands out as a philosophy centered on recognizing and nurturing a child's inherent strengths and positive qualities. Unlike deficit-based approaches that focus on correcting weaknesses, strength-based parenting aims to empower children, fostering their overall well-being and success. This essay explores the principles and benefits of strength-based parenting.

Central to strength-based parenting is the identification of a child's individual strengths. These strengths, spanning academic, artistic, interpersonal, and emotional domains, form the bedrock of this philosophy. By observing a child's interests, passions, and moments of success, parents gain valuable insights into their unique qualities. Once identified, these strengths become the focal point for encouragement, support, and opportunities for further exploration.

Strength-based parenting aligns seamlessly with the concept of a growth mindset, emphasizing the belief that abilities and intelligence can be developed through dedication and effort. This mindset, grounded in praising a child's efforts, perseverance, and progress, fosters resilience and a positive attitude towards learning.

Acknowledging and celebrating a child's strengths significantly contribute to the development of self-esteem and confidence. When children feel valued for their unique qualities, they approach challenges with a sense of self-assurance, creating a foundation for navigating life's complexities with resilience and determination.

Tailoring parenting strategies to align with a child's strengths is a distinctive feature of strength-based parenting. For example, if a child exhibits strong artistic inclinations, parents may prioritize providing opportunities for artistic expression and learning. Recognizing and accommodating a child's strengths in academic, social, and personal realms creates an environment where they can thrive.

Empowering children to make decisions based on their abilities and interests fosters autonomy and independence. This emphasis on a child's strengths contributes to a positive parent-child dynamic, where the child feels trusted and supported in their endeavors.

Strength-based parenting equips children with the tools needed to navigate challenges. By emphasizing their strengths, parents help children build a reservoir of resilience, enabling them to confront setbacks, learn from experiences, and develop problem-solving skills.

Fostering a positive and supportive parent-child relationship is a natural outcome of strength-based parenting. As parents actively engage with and appreciate their child's unique qualities, a sense of mutual understanding and connection flourishes. This positive relationship provides a solid foundation for effective communication and shared experiences.

The benefits of strength-based parenting are manifold. Children exposed to this approach are more motivated to engage in activities aligned with their strengths, fostering genuine enthusiasm for learning and self-improvement. Moreover, the emphasis on strengths contributes to emotional well-being, positive identity development, and the cultivation of effective coping strategies.

Identifying and Cultivating Your Teen's Strengths

The journey of parenting a teenager is a dynamic process of understanding and guiding them toward self-discovery and empowerment. One crucial aspect of this journey is identifying and cultivating the unique strengths inherent in your teen. This essay delves into the significance of recognizing these strengths and actively fostering their growth.

Identifying your teen's strengths involves a mindful and observant approach. Take note of their interests, passions, and areas where they naturally excel. This observation provides a foundation for recognizing the innate talents and attributes that make your teen unique. Whether it's academic achievements, artistic talents, interpersonal skills, or a combination of these, each strength contributes to their individuality.

Once identified, the next step is to actively cultivate these strengths. Provide opportunities and resources that allow your teen to explore and develop their talents. Whether through extracurricular activities, mentorship, or additional learning experiences, nurturing their strengths instills a sense of competence and accomplishment. Encourage them to set goals related to their strengths, fostering a sense of purpose and direction.

Moreover, it's crucial to acknowledge and celebrate their efforts and achievements. Positive reinforcement reinforces the belief in their capabilities and motivates continued growth. As a parent, your recognition serves as a powerful source of encouragement, bolstering their self-esteem and confidence.

In fostering a growth mindset, emphasize the idea that abilities can be developed through dedication and effort. Encourage a perspective that views challenges not as insurmountable obstacles but as opportunities for growth and learning. This mindset instills resilience and a positive attitude toward overcoming hurdles, contributing to a well-rounded and empowered individual.

The cultivation of your teen's strengths extends beyond individual accomplishments. It involves creating an environment that values their unique qualities and provides support for their aspirations. Foster open communication where your teen feels comfortable discussing their interests, goals, and challenges. This collaborative approach strengthens your connection with your teen and ensures that their strengths are recognized and supported.

In essence, identifying and cultivating your teen's strengths is a multifaceted process that requires sensitivity, observation, and active engagement. By recognizing their unique qualities and providing opportunities for growth, you contribute to their overall development and empowerment. As a parent, you play a pivotal role in guiding your teen towards realizing their potential and navigating the complexities of adolescence with confidence and purpose.

Encouraging a Positive Self-Image

Adolescence, marked by profound changes and self-discovery, underscores the critical importance of fostering a positive self-image in your teen. As a parent, actively contributing to the development of their self-perception becomes not only a supportive role but a crucial aspect of their overall well-being. This essay explores the significance of encouraging a positive self-image and provides insights into practical ways to nurture this fundamental aspect of your teen's identity.

The foundation of a positive self-image lies in acknowledging and reinforcing your teen's inherent worth. Express unconditional love and acceptance, emphasizing that their value is not contingent upon external achievements or societal standards. By consistently affirming their intrinsic worth, you provide a stable and secure base for the development of a positive self-image.

Actively engage in positive reinforcement by acknowledging and celebrating not only your teen's accomplishments but also their efforts and qualities. Focus on their strengths, talents, and the unique attributes that contribute to their individuality. This positive reinforcement serves as a powerful catalyst for building self-esteem and a resilient self-image.

In a world saturated with unrealistic beauty standards, fostering a healthy body image is crucial. Initiate open conversations about body image, emphasizing the importance of self-acceptance and self-care. Encourage a realistic and positive view of their bodies, highlighting the diversity of beauty. By promoting a healthy body image, you contribute to a positive self-image that transcends societal pressures.

Support your teen's journey of self-discovery by encouraging self-expression. Whether through artistic pursuits, hobbies, or personal style, provide a platform for them to express their identity. This sense of autonomy fosters a positive self-image as they learn to embrace and celebrate their individuality.

Establishing open communication channels is fundamental to encouraging a positive self-image. Create a judgment-free space where your teen feels comfortable expressing their thoughts, concerns, and emotions. Actively listen to their perspectives, validating their experiences, and providing guidance when needed. A supportive and communicative environment contributes significantly to a teen's sense of self-worth.

Help your teen navigate societal expectations and set realistic standards for themselves. Encourage them to focus on personal growth rather than comparison with others. By setting achievable goals and celebrating progress, your teen develops a positive self-image rooted in a sense of accomplishment.

Promote a growth mindset by emphasizing that abilities and intelligence can be developed through dedication and effort. This mindset encourages resilience in the face of challenges, as your teen learns to view setbacks as opportunities for learning and growth. Cultivating a growth mindset contributes to a positive and adaptive self-image.

In conclusion, encouraging a positive self-image in your teen is a holistic process that involves affirming their inherent worth, providing positive reinforcement, promoting a healthy body image, encouraging self-expression, fostering open communication, setting realistic expectations, and cultivating a growth mindset. As a parent, your role in shaping your teen's self-image is pivotal. By actively engaging in these practices, you empower your teen to navigate adolescence with confidence, self-assurance, and a strong sense of self-worth.

Part Four: Compassionate Discipline Strategies
  - Effective Discipline Techniques for ADHD Teens
  - Balancing Boundaries with Empathy

Part Four: Compassionate Discipline Strategies

Discipline is an essential aspect of parenting, guiding children toward responsible behavior and fostering their growth. However, the approach to discipline greatly influences a child's emotional well-being and the parent-child relationship. This essay explores compassionate discipline strategies, emphasizing the importance of empathy, understanding, and connection in nurturing a child's development.

Discipline is a fundamental component of parenting, shaping a child's behavior and character. In the realm of discipline, compassionate strategies stand out for their emphasis on understanding, empathy, and connection. This essay delves into various compassionate discipline approaches, highlighting their impact on fostering positive behavior and maintaining a healthy parent-child relationship.

Understanding Compassionate Discipline:

Compassionate discipline involves guiding children with empathy and understanding rather than resorting to punitive measures. It recognizes that discipline is not solely about correction but an opportunity for teaching, learning, and building a strong emotional bond between parent and child.

1. Positive Reinforcement:

Positive reinforcement is a key element of compassionate discipline. Instead of focusing solely on correcting negative behavior, parents actively acknowledge and reward positive actions. This approach reinforces desirable behavior, encouraging children to repeat actions that lead to positive outcomes.

2. Communication and Active Listening:

Effective communication and active listening play a pivotal role in compassionate discipline. By openly discussing expectations, consequences, and feelings, parents create an environment where children feel heard and understood. This fosters a sense of collaboration and cooperation.

3. Setting Clear Expectations:

Compassionate discipline involves setting clear and age-appropriate expectations for behavior. Children thrive when they understand the boundaries and expectations set by their parents. Clear guidelines provide a framework for positive behavior, reducing confusion and frustration.

4. Modeling Behavior:

Parents serve as powerful role models for their children. Compassionate discipline involves modeling the behavior parents wish to see in their children. Demonstrating patience, empathy, and effective problem-solving sets a positive example for children to follow.

5. Teaching Emotional Regulation:

Understanding and regulating emotions are crucial skills that compassionate discipline seeks to teach. Instead of punishing emotional expressions, parents help children identify and navigate their feelings. This approach empowers children to develop healthy emotional regulation skills.

6. Natural Consequences:

Compassionate discipline acknowledges that consequences are a part of learning. Instead of imposing punitive measures, parents allow children to experience the natural consequences of their actions whenever possible. This approach helps children connect their behavior with outcomes and learn responsibility.

7. Problem-Solving Together:

In situations where discipline is required, involving children in problem-solving encourages a sense of responsibility. Compassionate discipline includes discussions on why certain behaviors are not acceptable and collaboratively finding alternatives.

8. Time-In Instead of Time-Out:

Shifting from punitive time-outs, compassionate discipline incorporates "time-ins" where parents stay with the child during moments of distress or misbehavior. This approach fosters connection and provides an opportunity for the child to learn emotional regulation skills with parental support.

Effective Discipline Techniques for ADHD Teens

Disciplining teenagers with Attention-Deficit/Hyperactivity Disorder (ADHD) requires a thoughtful and nuanced approach that combines structure with understanding. This essay explores effective discipline techniques tailored for ADHD teens, aiming to foster positive behavior, self-regulation, and a supportive parent-teen relationship.

Disciplining teenagers with ADHD presents unique challenges due to their struggles with attention, impulsivity, and hyperactivity. Effective discipline techniques go beyond traditional approaches, emphasizing a balance between structure and understanding. This essay examines strategies that address the specific needs of ADHD teens, promoting their development and maintaining a healthy parent-teen dynamic.

1. Clear and Consistent Expectations:

Establishing clear and consistent expectations is fundamental when disciplining ADHD teens. Providing a structured environment with predictable rules helps them understand boundaries and reduces anxiety associated with uncertainty.

2. Positive Reinforcement:

Emphasizing positive reinforcement is crucial for teens with ADHD. Acknowledging and rewarding desired behaviors encourages motivation and self-regulation. Recognizing their efforts boosts self-esteem and reinforces the connection between positive actions and positive outcomes.

3. Constructive Communication:

Effective communication is paramount when disciplining ADHD teens. Engage in open and honest conversations to understand their perspective and express your expectations. Clear communication fosters trust and encourages teens to actively participate in problem-solving.

4. Break Down Tasks:

ADHD teens often struggle with organization and completing tasks. Breaking down tasks into smaller, manageable steps helps them focus and reduces the overwhelming nature of larger assignments. This approach supports their success and builds a sense of accomplishment.

5. Utilize Visual Aids:

Visual aids are powerful tools for ADHD teens. Use charts, schedules, and reminders to visually represent expectations and routines. Visual cues enhance their understanding, making it easier for them to follow directions and stay on track.

6. Implement a Reward System:

A structured reward system can be an effective motivator for ADHD teens. Establish a clear system where they earn rewards for meeting expectations. This system provides tangible incentives and reinforces positive behavior patterns.

7. Encourage Self-Reflection:

Encouraging self-reflection empowers ADHD teens to understand their actions and consequences. When they make a mistake, guide them in reflecting on the choices that led to it. This process promotes self-awareness and aids in developing better decision-making skills.

8. Provide a Safe Space for Emotional Expression:

Teens with ADHD may grapple with heightened emotions. Create a safe space for them to express their feelings without judgment. Encouraging open communication about their emotions helps them develop emotional regulation skills.

9. Collaborate on Solutions:

In disciplinary situations, involve ADHD teens in problem-solving. Collaboratively discuss the issues at hand and brainstorm solutions together. This approach fosters a sense of responsibility and encourages them to actively participate in shaping their behavior.

10. Flexibility and Patience:

Flexibility and patience are indispensable when disciplining ADHD teens. Recognize that their challenges may lead to occasional setbacks. Approach discipline with a long-term perspective, emphasizing continuous growth and improvement.

Balancing Boundaries with Empathy

In the intricate tapestry of human relationships, finding equilibrium between setting boundaries and expressing empathy is an art that shapes the essence of healthy connections. Boundaries, like gentle fences, define the limits of acceptable behavior and provide the structure for mutual respect. On the other hand, empathy ensures that these limits are communicated with a profound understanding of others' emotions and experiences. This essay explores the delicate balance required when navigating the intersection of boundaries and empathy, emphasizing the significance of nurturing connections rooted in respect, understanding, and shared humanity.

At the core of any healthy relationship lies the clarity of articulated boundaries. Whether in personal, professional, or familial spheres, transparent communication of expectations and limits serves as the bedrock for mutual respect. These boundaries create a framework that shapes the dynamics of interactions and sets the tone for the relationship.

Empathy serves as a guiding force when relationships extend beyond the boundaries, embracing the unique needs and experiences of individuals involved. Recognizing the diversity of perspectives, emotions, and backgrounds enables a compassionate approach to setting and respecting boundaries. It involves actively listening and acknowledging the validity of others' feelings, fostering a deeper connection.

Expressing boundaries with empathy necessitates mindful communication. Utilizing "I" statements to convey personal feelings and needs creates an atmosphere of empathy, emphasizing shared understanding rather than blame. The tone and manner in which boundaries are communicated significantly influence how they are received, shaping the overall dynamics of the relationship.

Central to an empathetic approach is the art of empathetic listening. Actively engaging in understanding another person's perspective fosters an atmosphere of respect and mutual understanding. Empathetic listening is a powerful tool in boundary discussions, demonstrating a genuine interest in the other person's experiences and contributing to a more collaborative approach.

While clear boundaries provide structure, an empathetic approach acknowledges the need for flexibility. Understanding that circumstances and emotions can vary allows for adjustments when necessary. This flexibility preserves the empathetic nature of the relationship, recognizing the dynamic nature of human interactions.

Emotions play a significant role in the negotiation of boundaries. An empathetic approach involves acknowledging and validating the emotions of both parties. Recognizing the emotional impact of boundaries fosters a sense of empathy and reinforces the human connection within the relationship.

Empathy thrives in an environment of collaborative problem-solving. When faced with challenges related to boundaries, addressing them as joint issues to be solved together enhances the connection between individuals. This collaborative mindset fosters a sense of shared responsibility and strengthens the fabric of the relationship.

Central to the balance between boundaries and empathy is a profound respect for personal autonomy. Acknowledging that individuals have the right to set and enforce their own boundaries creates an environment where each person feels valued and respected. This mutual respect becomes the cornerstone of healthy relationships.

In instances where boundaries are crossed, offering feedback with empathy becomes crucial. Instead of resorting to blame or criticism, providing constructive feedback focuses on finding solutions together. This approach maintains a sense of empathy even in moments of correction or adjustment.

At the heart of balancing boundaries with empathy is the creation of emotional safety within relationships. Knowing that one's boundaries are understood and respected creates a sense of security. This emotional safety fosters openness and vulnerability, strengthening the bond between individuals.

In conclusion, the art of balancing boundaries with empathy is a nuanced endeavor that requires intentional effort and mindfulness. By setting clear boundaries while understanding and acknowledging the emotions and needs of others, relationships can thrive in an atmosphere of mutual respect and connection. This delicate balance creates a foundation for healthy, supportive, and empathetic connections, fostering growth and harmony in human interactions. In navigating the intricate dance between boundaries and empathy, individuals contribute to the creation of relationships that not only endure challenges but also flourish in the shared understanding of the human experience.

Part Five: Academic Success Strategies
  - Collaborating with Teachers and School Staff
  - Implementing Homework and Study Techniques

Part Five: Academic Success Strategies

Attaining academic success is a multifaceted journey that requires dedication, effective planning, and a commitment to continuous improvement. This essay explores various strategies that students can employ to enhance their academic performance and foster a holistic approach to learning.

1. Goal Setting and Planning: Setting clear, realistic academic goals is the first step towards success. Break down large goals into manageable tasks, creating a roadmap for achievement. Develop a weekly or monthly plan, allocating time for studying, assignments, and other responsibilities. Effective planning enhances time management skills and reduces stress.

2. Active Engagement in Classes: Actively participating in class cultivates a deeper understanding of the material. Take thorough notes, ask questions, and engage in discussions. Actively engaging with course content during lectures reinforces learning and helps in retaining information.

3. Effective Time Management: Time management is a critical aspect of academic success. Create a schedule that prioritizes academic commitments, leaving ample time for breaks and other activities. Utilize tools like calendars or planners to stay organized and on track.

4. Utilizing Resources: Take advantage of available resources, including textbooks, online materials, and additional readings. Seek guidance from teachers, utilize tutoring services, and form study groups. Leveraging diverse resources enhances comprehension and provides a well-rounded understanding of the subject matter.

5. Healthy Study Habits: Cultivate effective study habits to optimize learning. Find a quiet, comfortable study space, eliminate distractions, and create a conducive environment. Break study sessions into manageable chunks with short breaks in between. Regularly review material to reinforce learning.

6. Active Participation in Extracurricular Activities: Engaging in extracurricular activities promotes a balanced lifestyle and contributes to personal development. Participation in sports, clubs, or community service fosters skills such as teamwork, leadership, and time management, which positively impact academic success.

7. Seeking Clarification: Don't hesitate to seek clarification on challenging concepts. Approach teachers, attend office hours, or collaborate with peers. Understanding foundational concepts is crucial for building a strong academic foundation.

8. Effective Note-Taking: Develop effective note-taking techniques during lectures. Organize notes logically, use keywords, and highlight key points. Reviewing well-structured notes facilitates easier comprehension and retention of information.

9. Prioritizing Self-Care: Prioritize physical and mental well-being. Ensure adequate sleep, maintain a balanced diet, and incorporate regular exercise into your routine. A healthy lifestyle positively influences cognitive function and academic performance.

10. Continuous Self-Assessment: Regularly assess your academic progress and adapt strategies accordingly. Identify areas of improvement, seek feedback, and make necessary adjustments to your study approach. Continuous self-assessment is a key component of sustained academic success.

Collaborating with Teachers and School Staff

Successful collaboration between students and educators is pivotal for creating a conducive learning environment. This essay explores the importance of fostering positive relationships with teachers and school staff and offers strategies to enhance collaboration for the benefit of academic success.

1. Open Communication: Establishing open lines of communication is foundational for effective collaboration. Students should feel comfortable expressing their thoughts, concerns, and questions to teachers. Similarly, teachers should encourage dialogue, providing a platform for students to voice their opinions and seek clarification.

2. Attend Office Hours: Actively participating in teachers' office hours fosters a deeper understanding of course material. It provides an opportunity for personalized clarification on challenging topics and allows students to build a rapport with their educators. Regular attendance demonstrates commitment to academic success.

3. Utilize School Resources: Schools often provide additional resources such as tutoring services, study groups, and academic workshops. Actively utilizing these resources enhances collaboration with school staff, ensuring that students receive comprehensive support beyond the classroom.

4. Seek Feedback: Actively seek feedback from teachers to understand areas of improvement. Constructive feedback helps students refine their academic approach, identify strengths, and address weaknesses. This collaborative exchange contributes to continuous improvement.

5. Participate in Parent-Teacher Conferences: For students in primary and secondary education, involving parents in the collaborative process is crucial. Attend parent-teacher conferences to discuss academic progress, address concerns, and work together to create a supportive learning environment.

6. Join Extracurricular Activities: Participating in extracurricular activities fosters collaboration outside the classroom. It provides opportunities to interact with teachers and school staff in different settings, strengthening relationships and creating a sense of community within the school.

7. Take Advantage of Online Platforms: Many schools utilize online platforms for communication and assignment submission. Regularly check these platforms for updates, announcements, and additional resources. Actively engaging with online tools demonstrates a commitment to staying informed and involved in the learning process.

8. Be Proactive in Problem-Solving: When facing academic challenges, be proactive in seeking solutions. Collaborate with teachers to identify strategies for improvement, discuss study techniques, or explore additional resources. Taking an active role in problem-solving demonstrates a commitment to academic success.

9. Attend School Events: Attend school events such as parent-teacher meetings, school assemblies, and educational workshops. These events provide opportunities to interact with teachers, administrators, and other school staff, fostering a sense of community and collaboration.

10. Demonstrate Accountability: Take responsibility for academic performance and actions. If challenges arise, openly discuss them with teachers and work collaboratively to find solutions. Demonstrating accountability strengthens the collaborative relationship between students and educators.

In conclusion, collaborating with teachers and school staff is a dynamic process that requires open communication, proactive engagement, and a commitment to mutual support. By actively participating in educational partnerships, students contribute to a positive learning environment, foster academic success, and develop essential skills for lifelong learning.

Implementing Homework and Study Techniques

The journey to academic excellence is paved with effective homework and study techniques. Establishing a consistent study routine is paramount, providing structure and discipline. Breaking down tasks into manageable segments alleviates overwhelm, fostering focused and efficient study sessions.

Active learning techniques, such as summarizing information in one's own words or teaching concepts to others, engage the mind dynamically. Prioritizing tasks using a to-do list ensures that essential assignments take precedence, maintaining order in the workload.

Experimenting with varied study environments allows students to discover optimal conditions for concentration and motivation. Leveraging technology wisely, taking mindful breaks, and reviewing material regularly contribute to a holistic approach to learning.

Collaborative efforts with peers in study groups enhance understanding through shared insights. Seeking clarification promptly when faced with challenging topics ensures a solid understanding, preventing misconceptions from persisting.

Designating a specific space for homework and setting realistic goals are integral components. Celebrating accomplishments along the way fosters motivation and a positive approach to learning.

In conclusion, effective homework and study techniques are fundamental to academic success. By incorporating these strategies into their routine, students not only optimize their learning experience but also develop essential skills that extend beyond academic realms. Consistency, engagement, and adaptability form the bedrock of a successful framework for homework completion and study sessions.

Part Six: Social Skills Development
  - Nurturing Healthy Friendships
  - Addressing Social Challenges and Bullying

Part Six: Social Skills Development

In the intricate dance of human connections, social skills play a pivotal role, shaping personal growth and enriching relationships. This brief exploration delves into the essence of social skills development and offers concise strategies for those seeking to enhance their ability to connect with others.

Effective communication, the bedrock of social competence, involves clear articulation, maintaining eye contact, and adapting to various contexts. It serves as the conduit for expressing thoughts, emotions, and perspectives. Active listening fosters empathy—an indispensable aspect of positive relationships. By understanding and appreciating diverse feelings and viewpoints, individuals contribute to a compassionate social environment.

Non-verbal communication, conveyed through body language and facial expressions, adds depth to interactions. Mindful consideration of one's cues and awareness of others' signals enhance the richness of social exchanges. Conflict resolution skills are essential, requiring constructive navigation of disagreements through techniques like active listening and compromise, contributing to harmonious relationships.

Building relationships necessitates intentional effort—initiating conversations, expressing appreciation, and dedicating time to nurture connections and create a supportive social network. Respect for diversity is fundamental, enriching relationships by acknowledging and valuing differing perspectives, cultures, and backgrounds.

Social confidence grows through stepping out of comfort zones, involving initiating conversations, attending events, and sharing thoughts with assurance. Teamwork and collaboration skills are essential, fostered through active participation in group activities and a positive contribution to team dynamics. Adaptability in social contexts, demonstrated through flexibility in communication styles and openness to new experiences, contributes to social success.

Understanding and adhering to social etiquette, encompassing politeness, consideration for others, and adherence to cultural norms, creates a positive and respectful social environment. In conclusion, social skills development is an ongoing journey that significantly contributes to personal growth and fulfillment. By actively cultivating these skills, individuals not only enhance their ability to connect with others but also contribute positively to the social fabric of their communities and workplaces. Social skills, beyond being tools for communication, serve as pathways to building meaningful relationships and navigating the complexities of the social world with grace and understanding.

Nurturing Healthy Friendships

In the intricate tapestry of life, friendships are vibrant threads that weave joy and support into our experiences. This essay explores the art of nurturing healthy friendships, offering concise strategies for those seeking to cultivate meaningful connections.

Authenticity is the bedrock of a healthy friendship, where being genuine and encouraging openness establishes a foundation for lasting and fulfilling connections. Mutual respect forms the pillar of any healthy friendship, valuing opinions, treating friends with kindness, and appreciating individuality to create a supportive and nurturing bond.

Communication is key to understanding and being understood. Open and honest dialogue, coupled with active listening, prevents misunderstandings and strengthens connections. Shared values and interests act as the glue binding friendships, with engaging in common activities and celebrating shared values deepening the sense of camaraderie.

Being a supportive presence in friends' lives marks a healthy friendship. Offering encouragement, lending a listening ear, and celebrating successes contribute to a positive and uplifting relationship. Establishing healthy boundaries is crucial, with respecting personal space, understanding limits, and communicating expectations creating a comfortable and secure environment.

Healthy friendships encourage personal growth, supporting aspirations, providing constructive feedback, and celebrating achievements to foster a dynamic and enriching connection. Conflicts, inevitable in any relationship, are signs of strength when resolved constructively. Openly addressing differences and working towards resolution strengthen the bond.

Embracing and celebrating diversity within friendships adds richness and depth. Appreciating unique qualities, perspectives, and backgrounds enhances the tapestry of social connections. Reciprocal relationships are fulfilling and sustainable, maintaining a balance in giving and receiving support, time, and energy for a sense of equality and fulfillment.

Cultivating healthy friendships is an art that demands authenticity, mutual respect, effective communication, shared values, and supportive presence. Establishing boundaries, growing together, resolving conflicts, celebrating diversity, and ensuring reciprocity contribute to the resilience and well-being of these precious connections. Friendships, when nurtured with care, become enduring sources of joy, support, and enrichment in life's journey.

Addressing Social Challenges and Bullying

In the intricate tapestry of human connections, social challenges and the pervasive issue of bullying cast shadows that impact individual well-being and erode the harmonious essence of communities. This essay delves into the imperative of confronting these challenges and advocates for a collective commitment to fostering a more inclusive and supportive social environment through empathy and understanding.

Understanding the Nuances of Social Challenges: Social challenges manifest in nuanced forms, from subtle exclusion to the overt pressures of conformity. Recognizing the diverse nature of these challenges is the initial stride toward crafting effective solutions.

The Unsettling Reality of Bullying: Bullying, a disturbing facet of social dynamics, encapsulates verbal, physical, or cyber aggression. Its insidious nature creates an environment of fear and distress, leaving indelible marks on mental health and societal harmony.

Profound Impacts on Individuals: The fallout from social challenges and bullying is profound, leading to emotional distress, shattered self-esteem, and a reluctance to engage in the tapestry of social interactions. Mitigating these impacts demands collective acknowledgment and intervention.

The Crucial Role of Schools and Communities: Schools and communities hold pivotal roles in addressing these issues. Robust anti-bullying programs, initiatives fostering inclusivity, and campaigns promoting empathy contribute to creating environments where individuals feel supported and secure.

Fostering Open Communication: At the heart of addressing social challenges lies open communication. Encouraging individuals to articulate their concerns, fears, and experiences creates an atmosphere of understanding, allowing for timely intervention and support.

Cultivating Empathy and Understanding: A compassionate society is cultivated through fostering empathy and understanding. Educational initiatives that champion tolerance, celebrate diversity, and teach conflict resolution serve as catalysts for positive social change.

Empowering Bystanders: Bystanders, often silent witnesses, can be empowered to play a pivotal role. Encouraging them to speak out, report incidents, and offer support creates a collective stand against social challenges and bullying.

Leveraging Technology for Positive Impact: In the digital age, technology is a double-edged sword. Harnessing online platforms to promote awareness, provide resources, and encourage positivity becomes an essential aspect in the fight against cyberbullying.

Legal Measures and Policies: A secure social environment necessitates the implementation and enforcement of legal measures and policies. Consequences for bullying behaviors, coupled with robust support systems, contribute to deterrence and protection.

Community Engagement and Support: Communities are the bedrock of societal well-being. Support groups, counseling services, and grassroots initiatives provide vital channels for individuals to seek assistance, find solidarity, and collectively combat social challenges.

In conclusion, the journey toward addressing social challenges and bullying demands a collective commitment from schools, communities, individuals, and society at large. By fostering inclusivity, promoting empathy, encouraging open communication, and leveraging technology responsibly, we can weave a social fabric where everyone feels valued and protected. Through these concerted efforts, we embark on a path toward a more compassionate and socially harmonious future.

Part Seven: Emotional Regulation Techniques
  - Coping Mechanisms for Emotional Rollercoasters
  - Teaching Stress Management and Self-Care

Part Seven: Emotional Regulation Techniques

In the realm of human emotions, the ability to understand, manage, and navigate our feelings is paramount for overall well-being. Emotional regulation techniques serve as essential tools to empower individuals in establishing a balanced relationship with their emotional landscape. This brief exploration delves into various strategies that enhance emotional intelligence and contribute to a more nuanced and resilient engagement with our emotions.

Emotional intelligence forms the bedrock of effective emotional regulation, encompassing self-awareness, self-regulation, and empathy. By cultivating a deeper understanding of our emotions, we lay the foundation for a more harmonious connection with ourselves and others.

Mindfulness and meditation offer powerful avenues for cultivating emotional regulation. By bringing focused attention to the present moment without judgment, individuals can navigate their thoughts and emotions with clarity, fostering a centered and calm mindset in the face of life's challenges.

Cognitive restructuring empowers individuals to challenge and reframe negative thought patterns. This technique enables a transformative shift in beliefs, paving the way for more positive and adaptive emotional responses to stressors.

Encouraging the healthy expression of emotions is vital for emotional well-being. Whether through creative outlets, journaling, or open conversations, finding constructive ways to articulate and process feelings promotes internal balance and authenticity.

Positive psychology provides a framework for building resilience by focusing on strengths and virtues. Cultivating optimism, gratitude, and a growth mindset contributes to a positive emotional framework, enabling individuals to navigate challenges with purpose.

Establishing healthy boundaries is integral to emotional regulation, delineating the space between self and others. By recognizing personal limits and fostering relationships built on mutual respect, individuals create a foundation for emotional stability.

Seeking social support from trusted individuals becomes a cornerstone of emotional well-being. This human connection provides an avenue for sharing emotions, gaining validation, and fostering a supportive network.

Regular exercise, effective time management, and relaxation techniques contribute holistically to emotional regulation. These practices, encompassing physical activity, organized schedules, and moments of intentional relaxation, serve as vital tools in managing stress and promoting emotional balance.

Coping Mechanisms for Emotional Rollercoasters

Life is an intricate tapestry woven with emotions that often resemble a rollercoaster – exhilarating highs and challenging lows. Coping with this emotional rollercoaster is an essential skill for maintaining mental and emotional well-being. In this exploration, we delve into effective coping mechanisms, providing individuals with tools to navigate the peaks and valleys of their emotional journey.

1. Resilience Development: At the core of coping with emotional rollercoasters is the cultivation of resilience. Resilience involves developing a mindset that views challenges as opportunities for growth. Embracing change, fostering a positive outlook, and building a robust support network contribute to resilience, enabling individuals to bounce back from adversity.

2. Emotional Awareness: Acknowledging and understanding one's emotions are fundamental to effective coping. Cultivating emotional awareness involves practices such as journaling, mindfulness, and self-reflection. These techniques empower individuals to recognize and navigate the nuances of their emotional landscape.

3. Healthy Coping Mechanisms: Engaging in healthy coping mechanisms is crucial for managing the intense emotions that accompany life's twists and turns. Constructive strategies include regular physical exercise, seeking social support, practicing relaxation techniques, and pursuing hobbies. These activities channel emotional energy in ways that contribute positively to mental and emotional well-being.

4. Adaptive Stress Response: Developing an adaptive response to stress is pivotal when facing emotional rollercoasters. This involves recognizing stressors, implementing effective coping strategies, and, when possible, altering the source of stress. Techniques such as cognitive restructuring, time management, and setting realistic expectations contribute to a more adaptive stress response.

5. Seeking Professional Support: In times of profound emotional turbulence, seeking professional support is a wise and courageous choice. Therapists, counselors, or support groups provide a safe space to explore and process complex emotions. Professional guidance offers valuable insights and coping strategies tailored to individual needs.

6. Artistic Expression: Artistic expression serves as a powerful outlet for navigating emotional rollercoasters. Whether through painting, writing, music, or other creative endeavors, individuals can channel their emotions into a form of self-expression. This not only provides a sense of release but also fosters a deeper understanding of one's emotional landscape.

7. Mindfulness Practices: Mindfulness practices, such as meditation and deep breathing exercises, offer moments of respite amid emotional turbulence. By grounding oneself in the present moment, individuals can create a buffer against overwhelming emotions, fostering a sense of calm and clarity.

8. Learning from Challenges: Embracing challenges as opportunities for growth is a transformative coping mechanism. Instead of viewing difficulties as insurmountable obstacles, individuals can choose to extract lessons and insights from their experiences. This shift in perspective contributes to resilience and a more empowered approach to emotional rollercoasters.

Coping with emotional rollercoasters is a dynamic and individualized process. By incorporating these coping mechanisms into daily life, individuals can navigate the peaks and valleys with greater resilience, understanding, and a proactive approach to their emotional well-being.

Teaching Stress Management and Self-Care

In the fast-paced and demanding landscape of modern life, teaching effective stress management and self-care practices is crucial for promoting mental and emotional well-being. This exploration delves into strategies aimed at empowering individuals with the tools to navigate stressors and prioritize their own self-care.

1. Mindfulness Practices: Introducing mindfulness practices forms a cornerstone of stress management and self-care education. Techniques such as mindful breathing, meditation, and body scan exercises equip individuals with tools to cultivate present-moment awareness. These practices contribute to a calmer mind, reduced stress, and an enhanced ability to handle life's challenges.

2. Stress Identification and Coping Strategies: Teaching individuals to identify stressors and implement effective coping strategies is essential. This involves developing awareness of personal stress triggers and introducing a repertoire of coping mechanisms. From problem-solving techniques to relaxation exercises, individuals learn to navigate stress proactively.

3. Time Management Skills: Time management skills play a pivotal role in stress reduction. Educating individuals on effective time management techniques enables them to prioritize tasks, set realistic goals, and create a balanced schedule. This not only reduces the pressure of deadlines but also fosters a sense of control over one's life.

4. Emotional Regulation Techniques: Understanding and regulating emotions are integral components of stress management. Education on emotional intelligence and regulation empowers individuals to navigate intense emotions, respond effectively to challenges, and maintain emotional well-being during stressful situations.

5. Healthy Lifestyle Choices: Promoting healthy lifestyle choices contributes significantly to stress reduction. Educating individuals on the importance of regular exercise, balanced nutrition, and sufficient sleep enhances overall well-being. These lifestyle factors play a crucial role in fortifying the body and mind against the negative effects of stress.

6. Self-Care Practices: Teaching self-care practices emphasizes the importance of prioritizing one's own well-being. From carving out moments for relaxation to engaging in activities that bring joy, self-care is a proactive approach to maintaining mental and emotional health. Encouraging individuals to establish self-care routines fosters resilience and a sense of self-nurturing.

7. Setting Boundaries: Establishing and maintaining healthy boundaries is a vital aspect of stress management and self-care. Education on boundary-setting involves recognizing personal limits, communicating effectively, and learning to say no when necessary. This skill enables individuals to protect their time and energy, reducing the risk of burnout.

8. Seeking Support and Community: Encouraging individuals to seek support from friends, family, or community networks is a crucial component of self-care education. Building a support system provides an outlet for sharing concerns, gaining perspective, and fostering a sense of connectedness, all of which contribute to stress resilience.

9. Reflection and Goal Setting: Teaching reflective practices and goal setting empowers individuals to assess their priorities and aspirations. By encouraging periodic self-reflection and the setting of realistic goals, individuals gain clarity on their values and can align their actions with their overarching life vision, reducing stress associated with conflicting priorities.

10. Continuous Learning and Adaptability: Stress management and self-care education emphasize the importance of continuous learning and adaptability. Life is dynamic, and individuals equipped with the skills to learn from experiences, adapt to change, and cultivate a growth mindset are better prepared to navigate stressors with resilience and a positive outlook.

In conclusion, teaching stress management and self-care is an investment in empowering individuals to navigate life's challenges with resilience and well-being. By providing practical tools and fostering a proactive approach to mental and emotional health, individuals can cultivate habits that contribute to a balanced and fulfilling life.

Part Eight: Supporting Independence

  - Gradual Release of Responsibilities

  - Preparing Your Teen for Adulthood

Part Eight: Supporting Independence

In the journey of personal development, supporting independence is a cornerstone that paves the way for individuals to flourish, learn, and navigate life's complexities. This essay explores the multifaceted aspects of supporting independence, acknowledging its significance in nurturing self-reliance, resilience, and a sense of purpose.

At the heart of supporting independence is recognizing and respecting the autonomy of individuals. Autonomy, the ability to make informed decisions and choices, empowers individuals to take charge of their lives. Whether in personal relationships, education, or professional endeavors, providing the space for autonomy is fundamental to the growth and development of an individual.

In the realm of education, supporting independence involves fostering self-directed learning. Encouraging individuals to take ownership of their education instills a lifelong love for learning and a proactive approach to personal and intellectual development. This process not only equips individuals with knowledge but also cultivates critical thinking skills and the ability to adapt to an ever-changing world.

In the professional sphere, autonomy is a catalyst for innovation and creativity. Supporting independence at the workplace involves entrusting individuals with responsibilities, encouraging them to take initiative, and providing avenues for professional growth. Empowered and independent employees contribute to a dynamic and thriving work environment.

Navigating the intricacies of personal relationships requires a delicate balance between support and giving individuals the space to make their own choices. Supporting independence within relationships involves recognizing and respecting each person's unique needs, aspirations, and boundaries. It entails fostering an environment where individuals can express themselves authentically and contribute to the relationship with a sense of autonomy.

Teaching independence to children is a crucial aspect of parenting. From early childhood, providing opportunities for decision-making and problem-solving instills a sense of responsibility. As children grow, supporting their independence involves gradually allowing them to take on age-appropriate tasks, make choices, and learn from both successes and failures. This process builds resilience and prepares them for the challenges of adulthood.

Supporting independence is intertwined with the development of emotional intelligence. Understanding and managing one's emotions, as well as recognizing and empathizing with the emotions of others, are essential components of independence. Emotional intelligence enables individuals to navigate social interactions, build meaningful connections, and make decisions that align with their values.

Embracing failure as a part of the learning process is integral to supporting independence. Encouraging individuals to take risks, learn from setbacks, and persist in the face of challenges fosters resilience. The ability to bounce back from failures is a testament to the strength of one's independence and determination.

Gradual Release of Responsibilities

The Gradual Release of Responsibilities (GRR) is an instructional model that aims to facilitate a seamless transition of learning responsibilities from teachers to students. This pedagogical approach recognizes the importance of systematically guiding learners through various stages of understanding and independence. The GRR model is often depicted in four phases: explicit instruction, guided instruction, collaborative learning, and independent learning.

1. Explicit Instruction:

In the initial phase, teachers take a prominent role in providing explicit instruction and modeling. This stage is characterized by clear explanations, demonstrations, and examples to introduce new concepts or skills. The focus is on ensuring that students have a solid foundation and understanding of the fundamentals.

2. Guided Instruction:

As students begin to grasp the content, the transition to guided instruction occurs. During this phase, teachers facilitate learning by working collaboratively with students. This may involve group discussions, interactive activities, and guided practice where teachers provide support and guidance as students apply their understanding in a structured setting.

3. Collaborative Learning:

The collaborative learning phase emphasizes interaction among students. Educators encourage collaborative activities and discussions where students work together to deepen their understanding. Teachers act as facilitators, guiding group activities, and fostering a cooperative learning environment. This stage promotes peer-to-peer interaction and shared exploration of the subject matter.

4. Independent Learning:

The ultimate goal of the gradual release model is to empower students to become independent learners. In the independent learning phase, students take on the majority of responsibilities for their learning. Teachers provide resources, projects, or assignments that allow students to apply their knowledge autonomously. This phase cultivates self-directed learning, critical thinking, and problem-solving skills.

Benefits of the Gradual Release of Responsibilities:

1. Cultivates Autonomy: The model fosters a sense of autonomy and ownership over the learning process, encouraging students to take charge of their education.

2. Supports Diverse Learning Styles: The gradual release accommodates diverse learning styles, ensuring that students receive the necessary support as they progress through each stage.

3. Encourages Critical Thinking: By gradually transferring responsibilities, students are prompted to think critically, analyze information, and apply knowledge independently.

4. Promotes Lifelong Learning: The emphasis on independent learning equips students with skills that extend beyond the classroom, nurturing a lifelong love for learning.

5. Differentiates Instruction: Teachers can tailor their support based on individual needs, providing additional guidance for those who require it and allowing others to progress independently.

Preparing Your Teen for Adulthood

The journey from adolescence to adulthood is a transformative period filled with challenges, growth, and self-discovery. As a parent, playing a pivotal role in preparing your teen for adulthood involves a multifaceted approach encompassing emotional, practical, and life skills. This essay explores key aspects of this preparation, emphasizing the importance of fostering independence, resilience, and a solid foundation for the transition to adulthood.

1. Nurturing Independence:

Encouraging independence is a cornerstone of preparing teens for adulthood. Provide opportunities for them to make decisions, solve problems, and take responsibility for their actions. This might involve managing their schedules, handling personal finances, or making choices about their education and career paths. Cultivating independence equips teens with the confidence and skills needed to navigate the complexities of adulthood.

2. Building Resilience:

Life is filled with uncertainties and challenges, and building resilience is a crucial aspect of preparing teens for the realities of adulthood. Encourage them to view setbacks as opportunities for growth, teach problem-solving skills, and emphasize the importance of maintaining a positive mindset in the face of adversity. Resilient individuals are better equipped to navigate the ups and downs of adult life with grace and determination.

3. Financial Literacy:

Equipping teens with financial literacy is an essential life skill. Teach them about budgeting, saving, investing, and responsible credit use. Introduce the concept of earning and managing money, whether through part-time jobs, allowances, or entrepreneurial endeavors. A solid understanding of financial principles prepares teens to make informed decisions about their economic well-being as they enter adulthood.

4. Effective Communication:

Communication is a cornerstone of healthy relationships and professional success. Help your teen develop effective communication skills, including active listening, expressing thoughts and feelings clearly, and understanding nonverbal cues. Effective communication fosters positive connections and empowers them to navigate the social and professional aspects of adulthood with confidence.

5. Time Management:

Balancing responsibilities and priorities is a crucial skill in adulthood. Teach your teen effective time management techniques, including goal-setting, prioritization, and creating a realistic schedule. Instilling these habits early on sets the foundation for responsible time management as they juggle academic, work, and personal commitments in adulthood.

6. Decision-Making Skills:

Adult life is rife with decisions, both big and small. Help your teen develop strong decision-making skills by guiding them through the process of weighing pros and cons, considering consequences, and making informed choices. Encourage critical thinking and problem-solving, empowering them to navigate the complexities of adulthood with confidence.

7. Emotional Intelligence:

Emotional intelligence is a valuable asset in personal and professional spheres. Teach your teen to recognize, understand, and manage their emotions. Emphasize the importance of empathy, self-awareness, and effective interpersonal relationships. Developing emotional intelligence equips them to navigate the social complexities of adulthood and fosters meaningful connections with others.

8. Goal Setting:

Encourage your teen to set short-term and long-term goals. This could include academic achievements, career aspirations, personal development, and more. Goal setting provides direction and purpose, instilling a sense of motivation and accomplishment as they progress through different stages of adulthood.

Part Nine: Cultivating Resilience Together
   - Parent-Teen Relationship Building
   - Celebrating Successes and Learning from Setbacks

Part Nine: Cultivating Resilience Together

The journey from adolescence to adulthood is a nuanced passage, demanding resilience in the face of evolving challenges. As parents, your role in preparing your teen for the intricacies of adulthood is paramount. This essay delves into the significance of cultivating resilience collaboratively, emphasizing the joint efforts required to empower your teen on their journey to maturity.

Resilience, in its essence, is the ability to rebound from adversity, adapt to change, and confront challenges with a positive mindset. As adolescents traverse the uncertainties and pressures of adulthood, cultivating resilience becomes a linchpin in equipping them with the emotional strength and coping skills necessary for this transformative period.

A foundational element in this process is open communication. Establishing an environment where your teen feels free to articulate their thoughts and feelings lays the groundwork for resilience. Actively listening without judgment, validating their experiences, and encouraging them to share concerns create a robust support system—an indispensable facet of resilience.

Setting realistic expectations becomes a guiding principle in this collaborative journey. Assisting your teen in delineating achievable goals and aspirations while emphasizing the inevitability of setbacks instills a sense of realism. This pragmatic outlook empowers them to approach challenges with equanimity, fostering resilience in the face of adversity.

Gradually entrusting your teen with more responsibilities and decision-making opportunities is a catalyst for building resilience. This gradual transfer not only boosts their confidence but also imparts the skills to make informed choices. Encouraging independence fosters a sense of self-efficacy—an integral component of resilience.

Problem-solving skills, closely entwined with resilience, become a focal point. Guiding your teen through practical problem-solving exercises encourages the analysis of challenges, brainstorming of solutions, and evaluation of outcomes. This proactive approach instills a mindset of resourcefulness and adaptability.

In the turbulence of adolescence, promoting emotional regulation is crucial. Assisting your teen in developing coping mechanisms for stress, anxiety, and disappointment establishes a foundation for emotional well-being. Practices such as mindfulness, deep breathing, or journaling can be effective tools in this endeavor.

Navigating failures and setbacks emerges as a defining facet of resilience. Encouraging your teen to perceive setbacks as opportunities for growth rather than insurmountable obstacles shapes their resilience. Sharing your own experiences of overcoming challenges underscores the lessons learned and the strength gained through adversity.

A growth mindset, emphasizing that abilities and intelligence can be developed through dedication and hard work, becomes a lodestar. This mindset nurtures a positive attitude toward learning and challenges, propelling resilience as your teen internalizes the belief that effort and perseverance pave the way to success.

The network of support plays a pivotal role in resilience. Encourage your teen to foster positive relationships with friends, mentors, and trusted individuals. These connections, characterized by emotional support and diverse perspectives, become pillars during challenging times.

As parents, your actions serve as a powerful influence. Modeling resilience in your own life, showcasing how you navigate challenges, cope with stress, and approach setbacks, becomes a tangible example. Your resilience becomes a beacon, illustrating to your teen that resilience is not merely an inherent trait but a learned skill.

Parent-Teen Relationship Building

In the delicate tapestry of the parent-teen relationship, understanding, empathy, and shared experiences weave the fabric that withstands the challenges of adolescence, laying the foundation for a lifelong connection.

Adolescence, a transformative phase, demands that parents grasp the nuances of their teens' perspective. It's a period marked by physical, emotional, and cognitive upheavals. Recognizing the innate need for independence and self-discovery becomes the canvas upon which a robust connection is painted.

Communication stands as the heartbeat of this intricate dance. It's not a monologue but a rich dialogue where thoughts, concerns, and experiences flow freely. Parents become adept listeners, fostering an environment of trust and mutual respect.

Setting boundaries becomes an art, a delicate negotiation between independence and responsibility. Clear expectations provide a framework within which teens can explore their autonomy. Negotiating these boundaries becomes a shared dialogue, ensuring a foundation of understanding and respect.

Engaging in shared activities becomes the thread that weaves the fabric of connection. Whether exploring hobbies, playing sports, or spending quality time, these shared experiences create a reservoir of memories, strengthening the ties that bind parent and teen.

Empathy emerges as a cornerstone in this intricate dance. Acknowledging the challenges and experiences of teens becomes a form of validation, creating a supportive atmosphere that affirms their concerns are heard and valued.

Nurturing independence is a delicate art. Parents become pillars of support, acting as a safety net while allowing their teens to explore abilities and learn from both triumphs and failures.

Parents, unwittingly, become the primary architects of their teens' understanding of relationships. The modeling of healthy interactions becomes a silent curriculum, shaping how teens approach relationships in their own lives.

Adaptability is key in the symphony of change that is adolescence. Parents become adept conductors, orchestrating responses to accommodate evolving needs and perspectives, ensuring the relationship remains resilient amid the challenges of growth.

Celebrating achievements becomes a ritual in the ebb and flow of adolescence. Recognizing the efforts and successes of teens serves as a form of reinforcement, encouraging them to pursue their goals with confidence.

The tapestry of the parent-teen relationship is woven through intentional understanding, empathetic communication, and shared experiences. This intricate dance, a synthesis of boundaries, support, modeling, adaptability, and celebration, is the foundation for a connection that not only survives the trials of adolescence but also evolves into a lifelong source of support and understanding.

Celebrating Successes and Learning from Setbacks

In the intricate tapestry of parenting, celebrating successes and guiding teens through setbacks emerges as a cornerstone in nurturing resilience. This narrative delves deep into the transformative power of these experiences, shaping not just moments but lifelong attitudes towards challenges and achievements.

Imagine the joy that fills a parent's heart when their teen achieves a milestone—be it academic excellence, artistic flair, or personal growth. It's not merely about the accolades but the journey that led to that moment. The late-night study sessions, the practice sessions filled with determination, and the self-discovery that unfolds with every step taken towards a goal—all these culminate in a celebration of hard work, perseverance, and resilience.

Celebrating successes isn't just about throwing a party or handing out trophies. It's about recognizing the effort, dedication, and growth that went into reaching that milestone.

It's a moment to pause, reflect, and acknowledge the strengths that enabled the achievement. A heartfelt congratulations, a thoughtful gesture, or simply a genuine expression of pride can work wonders in reinforcing positive behavior and motivating teens to continue striving for excellence.

However, life's journey is not always a smooth path. Setbacks, failures, and disappointments are inevitable companions in the pursuit of dreams. When faced with setbacks, such as a disappointing grade, a missed opportunity, or a setback in their aspirations, the true test of resilience begins.

As parents, our role in these moments transcends mere consolation or disappointment. It's an opportunity to teach valuable lessons in resilience, perseverance, and growth mindset. Instead of dwelling on the setback, we can guide our teens to reflect on what went wrong, what lessons can be learned, and how they can emerge stronger from the experience.

Setbacks are not roadblocks but stepping stones towards growth and learning. They offer a chance to build resilience, develop problem-solving skills, and cultivate a mindset that embraces challenges as opportunities for growth. Encouraging teens to identify their strengths, areas for improvement, and set realistic goals for moving forward empowers them to take ownership of their journey.

Sharing our own experiences of setbacks and how we navigate through them becomes a powerful teaching tool. It shows that setbacks are a natural part of life, and it's how we respond to them that shapes our resilience and character. By modeling resilience, perseverance, and a growth mindset, we inspire our teens to approach challenges with courage, determination, and a willingness to learn.

Creating a supportive environment where failure is not stigmatized but seen as a stepping stone towards success is key. Encouraging teens to seek support from mentors, teachers, or counselors, if needed, and reminding them that setbacks are opportunities for learning, adaptation, and personal growth fosters resilience and self-confidence.

Ultimately, the journey of celebrating successes and learning from setbacks is a transformative one. It's about nurturing a mindset that embraces challenges as opportunities, failures as stepping stones, and successes as milestones on a lifelong journey of growth and resilience. Through genuine praise, empathetic guidance, and unwavering support, we equip our teens with the resilience and mindset to navigate life's twists and turns with confidence and grace.

Raising Resilient ADHD Teen Boys by I Booky

Conclusion

The discussions surrounding the book "Raising Resilient ADHD Teen Boys: 9 Solutions for Parenting Teen Boys with Strength and Compassion" have been illuminating and insightful. From understanding ADHD in teen boys to exploring the importance of resilience in parenting, each topic has contributed to a comprehensive guide for parents navigating the challenges of raising ADHD teen boys.

The introduction sets the stage by highlighting the unique challenges faced by parents of ADHD teen boys and the importance of resilience in overcoming these challenges. It lays the groundwork for the solutions and strategies discussed throughout the book.

The subsequent chapters delve into understanding ADHD in teen boys, emphasizing empathy, and recognizing the challenges they face. It also covers practical approaches to building resilience, fostering open communication, setting boundaries, and encouraging independence while maintaining a supportive environment.

The book addresses the importance of celebrating successes and learning from setbacks, nurturing healthy relationships, and providing strategies for academic success and social skills development. It also delves into compassionate discipline techniques, effective discipline strategies, and supporting independence to prepare teens for adulthood.

Each chapter is infused with narrative elements, real-life examples, and practical advice to help parents navigate the complexities of raising ADHD teen boys. The discussions are not just about addressing problems but also about fostering resilience, self-confidence, and a positive mindset in both parents and teens.

In conclusion, "Raising Resilient ADHD Teen Boys" offers a holistic approach to parenting ADHD teen boys with strength and compassion. It empowers parents with the tools, strategies, and understanding needed to support their teens' growth, development, and well-being. By embracing resilience, empathy, and effective communication, parents can foster a nurturing environment that enables their ADHD teen boys to thrive and succeed in life.